AS IF THEY CAN BREAK

Pierce
St. Rose

ISBN: 978-1-967230-04-4

Cover by Pierce St Rose

Walnut Street Publishing
1673 South Holtzclaw Studio 14
Chattanooga, TN 37404
www.walnutstreetpublishing.com

as if they can break
companion album

available on all platforms

for
each
second
I am
privileged
to see
all
of
you

I

Porcelain Veins

Every step I take up this spiral
I firmly embrace those I love
Wrap around them a hundred times and step in song
Yet every step lands on the head of a soul I've never met

How can I feel peace for even a moment
When I witness the conscious slipping
Seeping through the seams of my skull
I see the wails ricochet these walls

This dining room is halfway up
Elaborate but not dignified
The plates just full enough to satisfy
We make mountains of them, then try to climb
And the fine china, we align in our godmind's design
Then tap-dance till the tea cups start to shriek

In the unwanted moment of clarity, I question if I try
Each of you carry me as much as I hold you
Catching the bits of porcelain as they fall
Watching wine drip from our skin in their wake

This time I spend praying to what I don't believe in
Pleading chaos to see reason
Why in this world, formed from the marrow of love's last rib
Am I hemorrhaging empathy daily?

Reality One

Reality One
Dream Two
Three graves
Reincarnation happens in four days
Tonight, a child saw it
Black shirt, blue jeans
Screaming in traffic
No crash
Lungs closing in
Reaction or blockage
Bystanders watch from the Rite Aid knoll
Am I one of them
Does it matter what I'm doing
Whether I'm in the backseat or the knoll
Or kneeling on the tarmac
Nothing would change
Tragedies you can't detain
Charge or sentence anyone for
Except god
This can't resurface
Four days later
I reach for a spoon
Excited to dig for dinosaurs in my oatmeal
Wet to the touch
Slugs in the drawer
That wasn't normal
How did I stop thinking about them

Years in doubt
They're back again
Did I push their sentencing out of my mind
Did I never know in the first place
It still can't resurface
Who will kneel by me when I'm gasping for air
Remember wishing it was a dream
I never knew how many funerals were held
This child doesn't know which reality won

Divinity

Waiting for the breakdown, there is no song playing
There is me looking at the giant inflatable ornaments
Hanging from the roof of this train station
Picturing myself slipping off one, and what then

Will they call me a poet
Will they call me a cigarette in Britain
Will they call me a graffiti scholar
A pitbull matador
Now I'm running like when I was six
Will I call myself a poet
Can I buy myself flowers before I wear my coffin as a jacket
When I hit the ground, I don't know what happens

It tests me now and then
It pulls the muscle beyond my skin
Headshots missing grey matter
I lied to the reflection, claimed I didn't care

Catholic religion and sinners' redemption
Peace forever and fundamentalist eye witness
Prostrate prayers and dark matter indifference
Fork-tongued fanatics and genuine priests
Most kind and hateful people I had no choice in meeting

Disregard conscious
Never place blame
Where I can place empathy
I know only two things
I love saying bitch
And I love being called it

One more I know
Every prayer I've made, the answer was no
Any wage gained was human and weighed,
And weighed
And weighed
On the hearts below
And below
And below
Those ornaments
This almighty tree sits

And I sit on something that used to be a pew
This moment is gentle
This moment is anger failed by apathy
Driven by lack of action
Driven by contentment with sweet nothings

I am dragged in chains to forward myself
By each of my past strangers
I was unable to avoid eye contact
My life is now yours

What will you call me?

After Leaving, The Shadow Stayed

What was the intent
After a drink
What was the intent
After a few more
The branches shadow
Mixed with their own
Finding our way home
No lamps in the car
Street lights cast this shadow
Sharply expressed
Affection, care, and abuse
Sit in the backseat, three abreast
Defense where there was no attack
I am no tank
I can't handle these shells
Rounds and rounds shot from their tongue
Cave in what little armor I wear
Scream to me and God and whoever is outside that door
How much you care for the air in these lungs
And when you saw I couldn't breathe
You came closer
And you shoved handwritten letters down my throat
Cut off any recovery
Apologize and rescind
Because your shadow is inseparable
The following phrase is usually said in condemnation
"Drunk words are sober thoughts."
You confirmed your intent
When you used that phrase as your only defense

Till then, we brushed off half truths
And made clever spins
I poured paint thinner on the blood you spilled
And I hardly have regrets
Because those that hurt me still need respect
Respect enough to be given time
Respect enough to be told
You've become a shadow cast by the one that hurt you
And respect enough to be left alone
When there's nothing else left
And even more
I'll always need help
Radical independence is theft
Radical independence is
Stealing the support we all breathe
Then pointing fingers when your wallet
Is the only one not empty
Everyone close to you is left a husk
And when you look in the mirror
Is it just a blur
Is it a foreign figure
Can you feel yourself
Driving around the culdesac
Can you find a way out
Can you not come to me when you do
My back is not a bridge to cross
And my legs can barely support myself
I cast my own shadows now
And if I don't pay their dues
Someone will write about me next

Life Diving

On this couch, every sound is tactile, and the cat makes
        biscuits on me
I struck a match, then lit a candle, then lit something that's
        not legal here
I could stay on this couch forever if they let me
        if I let me
I would sleep on this couch
And the bed in my father's house
And that floor I slept on before the concert
I'd live three different lives every day I wake
Whichever I see through
I'll find something different at the end

When I saw that mountain, mirrored in the lake
Snow shackled and sun spearing
It's knees as high as the hills I had known
When I saw that mountain, I wanted to climb it
After hiking a few miles, I decided
I had scaled it in one of those other lives
And didn't need to now

I write this lacking sleep after a red eye from Washington
I'm trying to avoid referencing that movie title
The scene when I landed wasn't catharsis or joy or regret
An emotion only described by the way the lamp shakes,
        the windows creak, and the ceiling rattles
The home hosting that couch looked almost like
        a wooden barrel at the bottom of the ocean
Holding nothing except the idea of lost treasure

I brought a few pieces with me, but they disappeared
        in my hand
        I want to dive in again
I know where I need to be in the future, but not now
        I want to dive in again
My soul could be in that barrel, or it might not be,
When I thought about it further,
        I forgot I was diving
        and hit my head on the pier

Looper

How many times
Fifty days on your mind
Twice a day
Sometimes five
Two hundred tally marks on my leg
The skin shreds
The trees start turning
The weather is cold again
How important is it
That I see it through this window
In my bed, in my home
In my disassociated nine-to-five
It persists against myself
This thought floats between every rock and wave
Of my white water brain

If spring comes and I'm still stuck in the ice
Paralyzed by the single thought
I would spend every season with you
And put it on loop
And put it on loop
Exchange this dead-end rumination
For a life I'd happily live two or three times
But even if I got what I want
It's not what I want
I have no ends
And I don't make plans
And I intend to keep it that way

Stopwatch Religion

and on the way home
she listened to them in this exact order

1. "Hey, Who Really Cares"
2. "Beautiful"
3. "Darling, I"
4. "squabble up"

this is how she pulls in

the driveway alone

again

again alone, she knows what love did
and didn't
and could or couldn't
and might, under the right conditions

if adrenaline can stand to take a seat
beat themselves down
drown in submission
time is her religion

time is her religion

her construct and her disdain
a fixture in her life not her regards
the pattern in her steps, the fog in the distance
on her wrist, on the bottom right of the taskbar
at the top left of the screenshot
the timer magnetically attracted to her granny's stovetop

in calm waters, the flame is steady
boiling overstimulation speeds up
what dopamine deficits eat up
the hands spinning again

now that she's alone again

everything she could be she saw in the distance
everything she wanted was always a figment
everything she needs is not in religious description

the facts hanging from flavor flav's neck
respect to the aging of the greatest things her great great
great great grandmother ever baked

as her soul washes away
she hopes the little affections she paid
paved the sidewalk for your head-clearing stroll today

this is how she pulls in

the driveway

alone again

darling who really cares, there's beauty in this reincarnation

this is how she pulls in

the driveway

again

Odyssey For An Iceberg
Cold Fear (2005)

Wake up, it's time for bed
Maintaining consciousness with a flat tire on their neck
The air screams out of their mouth with no sound
Circumstance drains the sleep from their sleep
So they dream in daylight

They looked for a soul at the end of a rainbow,
        but there was only a pot of gold
They looked for a fire inside but preferred the cold
Cold enough to freeze the hairspray in their braids,
        and the tears on their knuckles

They broke out a lighter for warm reprieve and then,

They looked for a reason to live, plowing deep into southern
        snow
And when the shovel broke, they dug, and they dug, and they
        dug
Ice and mud in the fine line between their fingerprint and their
        nail
And when their nails cracked
        they ate the snow
As it melted
        they drank the snow
In frozen hands and trembling lips,
        they found another home in the cold

That all happened at my desk chair
Because we don't get snow here anymore

I felt like I should feel more at that mountain from before
I felt like I wanted to slide down the valley and use the
      mountain peaks as ramps
Soaring high enough to punish the eagles for stealing
      other birds' prey
But that's our mascot and our flag, and what better
      representation could we have
Tired again, I pass life to the inside of my eyelids
My hands frozen
Lashes frosted
Beneath all the snow
Underneath the bedrock
I found the tip of an iceberg
So I reach to my pocket for my lighter
      and the shelf for my hairspray

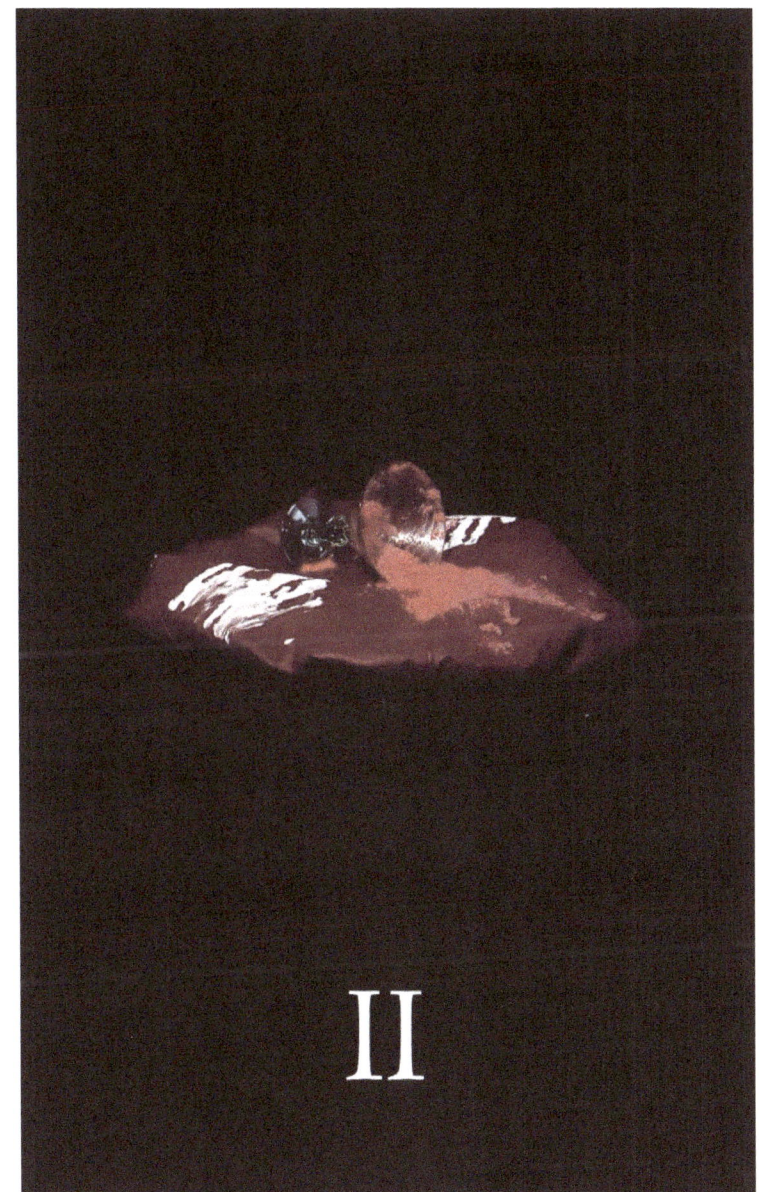

II

Canned Biscuit Surprise

Pop-Tarts in the toaster
Lightning from the sky
Or the ground
It's scary either way
Fireworks, at least, are pretty
Canned biscuits are scary
Like a jack in the box
Some of these have control; some don't
Every morning
Day after day
Get mom to press the spoon down on the biscuits
Pop
Tots cold in the cafeteria
Chalk rolling on the floor
The test doesn't matter now
They didn't expect a drill today
Don't bump your head on the way
Under the desk, pray no pen drops
Red and blue strobe through the window
But never move closer
Pop
Some stifle sobs
And hope the door doesn't open
The seconds are hours, a week passes in a blink
Returning to their desk
Next to so many empty seats
On the TV in their home
Atop the crayon-stained cabinet, strangers argue
A time for grieving, a time for change
A time for prayer, a time for love

Mom cuts it off
And secures another hug
Sunlight passes through the curtain onto the cabinet
The bottom shelf dusty
The army men look different
They are hungry
They walk to the kitchen
And open the biscuits
Pop

Barrel

Empathy in crashing economies is commodity
They told the little one to shoot for their visions
And raised them to shoot at anything that doesn't match
The clip is spent

Their sky has been poisoned since before they laid eyes on it
They are lost in the empty chamber
March with the others, off the smoking barrel's edge
Or hide and let them fall

Hide under the tallest tree
Let the sap wash over
Petrify all their armors
Toys, weapons, and tools

All they needed was a rock
Steady hands
And good aim
Or a lot of rocks

Take Your Seat

This moment right now
Is paradise
And I'm sorry
Your best shot at tuition is from half-court,
But your seat number is wrong
Your best shot at rent is a scratch off,
All you receive is foil under your nail
You go back to work,
And the feeling follows you

You are sitting in a cuck chair

Every waking hour off, you spend on yourself,
On a future that matters
And after every jeer and applause
After the sweat and the hugs
After all your penny-pinching and self-care spending
It all comes down to Friday night
It's you, a ball, and forty-six feet

A man who works can hardly eat
A man who does not work—

Honey comes at a cost
It runs from our veins like water,
And cycles into the clouds they watch us from
Harvest the little delight left in our present,
And bring us forth prostrate, thinking of furnished homes

I have never seen a starving executive officer

In Your Service

My fate is to scribble fine poetry on my brain
During the downtime from two-to-five
And forget the passages by six
To paint murals with sauce packets on my lunch break
Then throw away the canvas with the rest of the plates

My fate is to go on ill-advised dates with those bold enough
To ask a human who is trapped
Regret abounds after the car ride guided by jack and coke,
And also coke

Another cried freedom
I hope they opened that bed and breakfast
Maybe I could work there instead
But there are so many to serve here and now

From 10-10

We should keep a gun on hand,
Not to protect the registers
But for the next ▓▓▓ that starts their order with
"Uhhhh, one second."
For the next ▓▓▓ that asks for no ice at the window

10-10

Almighty God of nothing I perceive,
Strike down the gaslighters
The old man said I didn't give him his 25 cents change
That is destined to change his life
I reject his sweet lies

We have a camera over the register
And a camera in the hall, and at drive
Asset protection's all-seeing eyes

10-10

We are at your service
Is that all?
Would you like to round up for the
Childrenscollegehospitalflooding fund?
No problem
Your total is 6.66
Have a nice day

Cruelty's Prayer

All the joy he stole from our purses

I cast aside, for a moment, and send a dream

Of walls and fences face down

Of the softest pastels embracing burgundy stained-towns

Of wolves and sheep protecting the hen's eggs

Of soil and sky tended by metal hands

Of passion and rest, of passion and rest

Of concern for my sister I have never met

I sent a dream to him

And received nothing

Who Loves You Today

At what story does stepping out of a window go from
          a whimsical exit to self harm
Consume until my stomach is sick,
          and give until my hands cramp
Bored of hedonism,
          bored of philanthropy
These thoughts aren't filling,
          and these fidgets are failing me
The gas pump won't click

How long will this distraction last

How can I distract myself when I can't swim in the lake
          without plastic penetrating my pores
How can I distract myself for a day
          when every distraction costs a week's wage
How can I distract myself when I don't care for fate or destiny
          or whatever my soul is supposed to be
How do I stop thinking about what I stand on
          and who is standing on me

If I can't stop,
          how do I start

Cop City

Cop City has surrounded its first criminal

Before its roads were built
And fake walls erected
Or plastic apple pies baked
The trees must fall
For the trees to fall, the land must be cleared
For the land to be cleared
A man sitting cross-legged must be removed

Cop City has surrounded its first criminal

We planned into failure, shouting at brick walls
We wished our tax dollars had gone to a new stadium
The lights only flash red now, his skin solid blue
How can one hold a gun with bullet holes in their palms
They nail us down and carry out crucifixions daily
Without the courage to address their ward or turn on a camera
Without the will to look themselves in the mirror afterward

Cop City has found its first victim

Dirty South (1995)

When his followers scarred their soul
He did not answer their call
Bible belt whip you raw

In the south, you could throw stones anywhere
And hit a queer preacher's kid, or two
And they do

Before sunrise, I flew
I tried to acquire everything money can't buy
While you beat on the empty pinata

A coffin with bullet holes in it
Or that one summer, a rose-tinted menace
Pedestrians can't tell the difference
Between you at your cleanest or most dented
Because those shades hide the blues and greys

While having few griefs and fewer greens
They paved their way with concrete spilling from each ear
And railings built by their worst fears
The trail lit with their brightest ideas

And I recall every cheers

And I recall every cheers

And the faces and their hatred and the years
Show themselves as the scar on my brow heals

Further every cheer

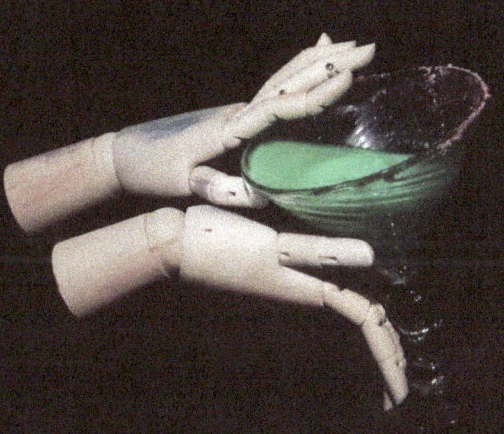

III

Golden Lake Loop

If I believed in God, I wouldn't pray, because I couldn't ask for
anything more

5 days ago, I touched the ground
Black cherry on my lips
4 days ago, I fell asleep in the comfort of friends
And gay vampires on the television
3 days ago, I saw a clown driven to murder
I was that clown once, but I didn't stab anyone
2 days ago, I was proud of you
2 days ago, I was proud of me
1 day ago, we booked a train to the wrong place
And missed it anyway
I hope 1 day isn't too soon to joke about it

Everything I know, I know from contradiction
Everything I love, comes from imperfection
We missed a train and found a waterfall
We didn't find shrooms but we found a damn fine cherry pie
We stayed inside our border and stumbled into a golden lake
1 lake of hundreds of lakes, peaks, trails, vistas, beaches,
and mountains within the width of my thumb
Pressed against this map

Contentment has been elusive in each of these 23 years
Yesterday I felt it
I felt peace eating a service berry off the branch
I felt peace tracking the foot of the mountain to the fog
obscuring its peak
I felt peace running my hands on the water, clearer
than the mud I come from

Agent Cooper came to me in a dream and told me I feel
nostalgia for this land I've never seen because I've never felt
peace in the present, only in the good of my past
Yet I felt peace walking with you
If I've ever felt this peace before
I was too young to recall it now
Every time I've touched contentment
The bubble popped before me
The mist hit my face, and I kept walking
This time, the only thing testing my peace is the knowledge
that it has to end

But today, even that slipped my mind
We crossed oceans and climbed mountains
We were called slurs that only validated us further
I'd be jealous if I saw me too
Even more if I saw me next to you
Each time we stop to take a picture, you ask if your hair is okay,
Each time I say "Always."
I felt peace talking from there and back
It's difficult to be myself
It's harder when I've already shown my repressed self
What if they only like the veil and not the face behind it
But you already know who I am
You try to imagine what I'd be like if I was angry
How delicate would I be then?
You said I "Handle things as if they can break."
I don't know why that makes me tear up
More than the peak of this mountain
More than the deer grazing at my feet
I lay here overwhelmed, knowing only 1 or 2 embraces are left
until we part again

1 day later, I travel from the hairline of this country to the soles of its feet
This still dominates my soul
My feet are in the sand
My eyes observe more nature I've never seen
But it isn't the same
I've never felt this for a land
I've never felt this for a friend
I've never thought it romantic
I said that would be unnatural
And maybe that's right
Or maybe that's a lie I tell myself
Or maybe it's both and neither, and this kind of comfort is a feeling I don't know how to feel yet
I'm used to Roman candles
This is a bonfire
Every experience is another log stacked caringly on the flame
Every conversation is a flickering cinder returning to its earth
And maybe the bonfire was lit two years ago
When you grabbed my arm and I thought

If I believed in God, I wouldn't pray, because I couldn't ask for anything more

Light // Guiding

I held on to that little joke they told

the all-important stone or weapon or salve

given to me on a journey

is it the only thing to save this world

//

my world is built on the meeting of the sand and the trees

where the sticks make walking barefoot more uncomfortable
than I'd like

I still walk

and I still remember my future fondly

The Top Left Bottom Drawer

What am I looking at this person for
That feeling
Six years old, the one time a year we moved the fridge to clean
I found my lost bouncy ball
That feeling

What am I talking at these people for
They enchant and embrace
Yet when I return to the picture laid face down
I reach my hand in and feel the creases on my face
They are spelling joy
A joy only a sea of trees can provide

What am I looking at these people for
They laid in my palms
When the eyes on my kneecaps saw Sodom
They understood how sad a frown must feel
When it's time to smile again

What am I holding this person for
That feeling
The first two weeks of your first person
When everything is going to be okay forever
That feeling

I yearned
After receiving all I wished for

Grossly Intact

The after-visit summary said my behavior was restless
and fidgety
Red lights and loading circles are the same to me
My brain keeps running when the world stops

I feel the weight of my thoughts tipping my head over
My neck is stuck staring down my future on a brush
The hairs make small space for serenity in my skull

It's either too much or not enough
So I spill over my own cup
Drifting through the apex
Or spinning off the road

I met them for the third or fourth time in that ditch
I still doubted their name, their face, their life
I may have thought you were two or three other people

Every moment, every thought I could have comes and goes
at the same time
Trying to skip too many stones at once
Guessing which one will make it to the other side

The after-visit summary said my cognition was grossly intact
And I couldn't agree more
You know this is how my brain works, and you still ask me for
a five-year plan
Can't I be happy now?

Chewing On The Pit

There is a melon where their head used to be
There is a melon
So much in such a small time
After a few spins around the sun
No one would know
Least of all me
There is an orange on their corner
Where I came and went after paying my daily debt
There is an orange where they let me rest
Another spin
Rarely reach for the question
Are they still alive?
The last time we spoke, there was a grape
In the palm of my hand
There is a grape
They reach for me, palms filled with sweat and tears
My fingers turn themselves inside out
Layer by layer
A matter of nature
This void is protected
There is nothing they can do about that now
Blood and bones escaping
Lemon zest and spilled wine fill the creases
Reading my hand
As I stain this small peeling globe
Dust hugs my fingertips
I spin again

How to Win Friends and Influence People (1936)

My greatest strength is wielding as little as I can
My last demand was requesting rebate on the water that
        washed over my crown
Exercising powers above to exorcise demons below
        now, I address those spirits as friends
Not in dramatized lyrics or ritual circles
        I mean it like a turn signal
Blinking left and right at the same time
It's the hazard I love, the reason you pulled over

Would any notice if my lights were off?
Dusk to dawn pile-ups and blood drawn
The thread isn't gone; It's turning the corner
        no dynamics or expectations
And if you start to get one, I might turn it around
        then turn it back around
I'll only fuck up in endearing ways because power isn't a play
But we can talk about the fortes of my younger days or
        stress-eating seasoned pretzels in depressive states
We can meet when the tide is slack, follow the seagulls' tracks
        we don't need floodgates

Heaven is high water
Heaven is high water
This river changes every day but will remain running for you to
        float away
I maintain, hold me, and I will hold you always
I maintain
This river changes every day but will still be still enough for
        you to stay

Hail Mary

Pushing ninety now
Three kids, maybe four; I can't remember
One of them you don't talk to anymore
Two of them became preachers
One of those became my father
She's been gone only a few years
You've been abhorrent for all I've breathed
How old were you when you had your first child
How old was she when she gave birth to them
Now, pushing ninety,
You tell each of your children
"I know what kind of person I am. I know I don't have much
time left. Tell me what do to different, I don't want to go to
hell."
A full court shot at the buzzer
Launching scripture from outside the stadium
You give new meaning to Hail Mary
But you're not a gunslinger or the sheriff
You can't change yourself solely for yourself
At the twelfth hour
You are not entitled by law to their time and love

Still, two of your kids respond
Because you were once a dad
One told me you were different in your prime
Another doesn't know what happened to you
A day in your home feels like a toothless pitbull gnawing on
their ankles, a declawed cat swatting infinitely
Pure vitriol with no strength or conviction to back it up
It's past nihilism or christian guilt
And it's not particularly political
An old, brittle man, self-imposed lonely

A man who needs everyone around him
To feel his hate for living
Now you want to turn on a dime
You stepped on every one of them up until now
Marching to a funeral where the evangelist will be the only
person in attendance

Your daughter encouraged you to have the surgery
When the leaves started to turn, you did
And by the time they fell,
You said you'd never forgive her for it
Because it's keeping you alive longer
The truest words you have said
You are the victim, time again, the victim of children
Who came to you because you have too much pride
To admit you can't care for yourself
The victim of children who care for you because they can't
burn leeches off unless the lord tells them to
You've had ninety years
I don't know who hurt you
I don't know what made you this way
I don't care anymore
Talk to God about it
Take your shot
I know where you're going

What's Heaven to You

eyelids part peacefully
observe the ceiling
splattered with purple paint, dripped and dried
I don't know where I am but it feels safe and uncomfortable,
soothing and new
the next room has no screens, no monitors
one piece of furniture
I can't tell if it's a stool or a table
I accept a stool is a small table we decided it was okay to put
ourselves on instead of food

I walk into the next room without thinking
this room has a single speaker at its center
it's playing ADHD, Int'l Players Anthem, and Shot You Down
a phone is in the corner, it's not mine,
yet it has all the numbers I need
I call and tell you if you blink you'll be in this room too,
you do, and you are
I give a careful hug, as close as I can muster, as gentle as
unsteady hands can manage
if either of us breaks, we can fit the pieces back almost right
and try again

we pick up the phone and laugh with those in it
and laugh about those who aren't
I say a prayer to myself
and I am happy

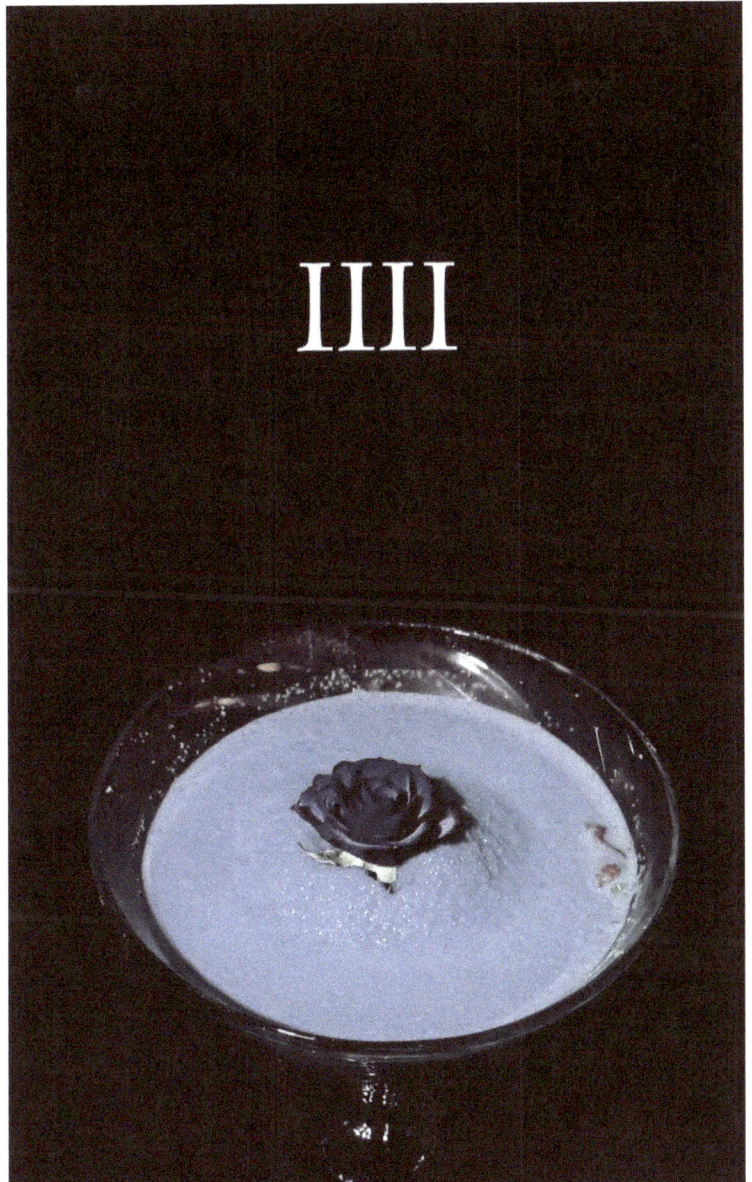

The Most Important Part Is You Leave Home

What feeling captures the most confident, calm, present,
distant, anxious, and uncertain state

The feeling when the roads that are your only world have
been driven into the earth

The feeling when the persons you claim as yours can't follow
you past those roads

The feeling when you don't know a quarter of the destination
you are going to call home

I'm sure of this feeling,
I would sell my soul for a misadventure carrying the chance of
a replacement for said soul

Whether a person, a mountain, a purpose, or that feeling when
I sit on the floor at the end of my day

And know that I have done all I could

In that feeling,
I have loved all that I needed to love
And hugged all that I needed to hug

That feeling tells me if I die in my sleep tonight
And see each of those I love one last time
Through the eyes in my ashes and mouth of my urn

Every one of them would understand

I did not let regret break my spine

I can't experience all that I believe is fulfilling

They're all in different places and fading and moving and
dying and being created in the corners of the earth I have seen
and many I will never see

Now understanding to live my life fulfilled all I need
Is to catch each experience as they pass me
And hold onto them as long as we need to be held

At that point, letting go is fulfilling as all else

In that mind, I wrote to you in August
To each of those I have met and will meet
And to every river I wade and sky I cross

August 15th,
Three hours till the metal detector
And the awkward in-between
The display on the seat in front of me is broken
There is nothing to distract me from my choices
And I will sit with them as friends would
Eating in a parking lot at 3 am
On shuffle, she sings in choir
"Funny how time flies when you're having fun,
please stay."
I promise I'll leave and return, and leave and return,

and leave

and leave

I promise

As If
They Can
Break

All my thanks and love to
Aaron Quinn,
for innumerable moments of creativity and friendship
Blake Hurst,
for serving as an editor, brother, and friend
Rachel "Krums" Krumenacker,
for editing (and friendship)
five to fifty more names;
it would seem obnoxious to list you all,
if you know you know,
and you know that I love you.